*Discovering Ant*ㅤㅤㅤㅤㅤㅤ*...de Travel*
Guide

Antalya

Travel Guide

2023

Josefina B. Zimmerman

Table of Contents

I. Introduction

Overview of Antalya

Antalya is a captivating coastal city located on the southwestern coast of Turkey. It is the largest city on the Turkish Mediterranean coast and serves as a gateway to the Turkish Riviera. With its rich history, stunning natural beauty, and vibrant atmospheres, Antalya attracts millions of visitors each year.

Geographical Location

Situated on the Gulf of Antalya, the city enjoys a privileged location between the azure waters of the Mediterranean Sea and the majestic peaks of the Taurus Mountains. Antalya's unique geography offers a breathtaking backdrop of mountains and sea, creating a picturesque setting for travelers.

Historical Significance

Antalya has a long and storied history that spans over 2,000 years. The region has been inhabited since ancient times and has witnessed the rise and fall of various civilizations, including the Hittites, Romans, Byzantines, and Ottomans. As a result, Antalya boasts an impressive collection of archaeological sites, ancient ruins, and historical landmarks that showcase its rich heritage.

Modern City Life

While Antalya proudly embraces its historical legacy, it also thrives as a modern and cosmopolitan city. The city center blends the old and the new, with narrow winding streets of the historic Kaleici (Old Town) district juxtaposed with modern shopping malls, luxury resorts, and bustling nightlife. Visitors can immerse themselves in the vibrant street life, explore traditional markets, indulge in delicious cuisine, and experience the warmth and hospitality of the locals.

Tourism and Attractions

Antalya is renowned for its pristine beaches, crystal-clear turquoise waters, and an abundance of natural wonders. The region offers a wide array of outdoor activities, including swimming, snorkeling, scuba diving, hiking, and boat tours. Additionally, Antalya is home to several well-preserved ancient cities, archaeological sites, and museums, allowing travelers to delve into the fascinating history and culture of the region.

Climate

Antalya enjoys a Mediterranean climate characterized by hot, dry summers and mild, wet winters. The city experiences over 300 days of sunshine annually, making it an attractive destination throughout the year. Summers are ideal for beach activities and water sports, while the cooler months provide pleasant conditions for exploring historical sites and engaging in outdoor adventures.

In the following chapters, we will delve deeper into the cultural heritage, geographical features, climate, and attractions of Antalya, offering you a comprehensive guide to make the most of your visit to this enchanting city.

History and Culture

Antalya is steeped in a rich history that spans thousands of years. From ancient civilizations to the influence of various cultures, the city has a diverse cultural tapestry that is reflected in its architecture, traditions, and way of life. In this chapter, we will explore the historical significance and cultural heritage of Antalya.

Ancient Civilizations

The history of Antalya dates back to antiquity, with evidence of human habitation in the region as early as the Paleolithic era. Throughout its history, the city has been under the influence of several prominent civilizations. The Hittites, who ruled Anatolia during the 2nd millennium BCE, were among the early inhabitants of the area. Later, the region came under the control of the Persian Empire and then the ancient Greeks.

One of the most significant periods in Antalya's history was during the Roman era. Under Roman rule, the city thrived as a major port and trade center. Magnificent structures such as Hadrian's Gate, the Antalya Roman Harbor, and the ancient theater of Aspendos were constructed during this time.

Byzantine and Ottoman Influence

With the decline of the Roman Empire, Antalya came under Byzantine rule in the 5th century CE. The Byzantines left their mark on the city with the construction of fortifications and churches, some of which can still be seen today. The Byzantine era lasted until the 13th century when Antalya was captured by the Seljuk Turks.

During the 14th century, the city became part of the Ottoman Empire. Under Ottoman rule, Antalya experienced a period of growth and development. Many mosques, hammams (Turkish baths), and caravanserais were built, adding to the architectural richness of the city.

Cultural Heritage

Antalya's cultural heritage is a tapestry woven with influences from its diverse history. The city embraces both its ancient roots and the traditions of its modern Turkish identity. The locals take pride in preserving and celebrating their cultural heritage through various means.

Traditional arts and crafts are an integral part of Antalya's cultural fabric. Skilled artisans create exquisite handwoven carpets, ceramics, and woodwork, showcasing the region's artistic prowess. Visitors can explore traditional markets and bazaars, such as the Old Bazaar (Kaleici Pazari), where they can witness the craftsmanship firsthand and purchase unique souvenirs.

Cultural festivals and events are celebrated throughout the year, offering a glimpse into the local traditions and customs. From music and dance festivals to religious observances, these events provide opportunities for visitors to immerse themselves in the vibrant cultural scene of Antalya.

Gastronomy

Antalya's culinary scene is a reflection of its cultural diversity. Traditional Turkish cuisine, with its rich flavors and aromatic spices, takes center stage. The city is renowned for its fresh seafood dishes, grilled meats, mezes (appetizers), and delectable desserts.

Exploring Antalya's restaurants and cafes provides a culinary journey through Turkish flavors. Whether it's enjoying a traditional kebab, savoring a plate of freshly caught fish, or indulging in the famous Turkish delight, the gastronomy of Antalya is sure to delight food enthusiasts.

As you explore Antalya, you will encounter the remnants of its historical past and experience the vibrant cultural scene within the city. The fusion of ancient ruins, architectural marvels, traditional crafts, and gastronomic delights makes Antalya a captivating destination for history enthusiasts and cultural explorers alike.

Geographical Features

Antalya's geographical features are diverse and captivating, offering a picturesque backdrop to the city and its surroundings. From stunning coastal landscapes to majestic mountains and natural wonders, the region's geography contributes to its unique charm. In this chapter, we will explore the geographical features that make Antalya a remarkable destination.

Coastal Landscape

Antalya has a beautiful coastline along the Mediterranean Sea. The turquoise waters, sandy beaches, and rocky cliffs create a breathtaking setting. The region boasts a variety of beaches, ranging from popular and lively to secluded and tranquil.

Konyaalti Beach is one of the most well-known beaches in Antalya. Located west of the city center, it offers a long stretch of pebbly shoreline with stunning views of the Taurus Mountains. Lara Beach, situated to the east, is famous for its sandy shores and luxurious beach resorts. These and other coastal areas provide opportunities for swimming, sunbathing, and enjoying various water sports.

The Taurus Mountains

The Taurus Mountains form an impressive backdrop to Antalya, enhancing its natural beauty. These mountains stretch across the region, creating a scenic panorama. The rugged peaks, deep valleys, and pine-covered slopes offer excellent outdoor activities and exploration opportunities.

The mountains are a haven for hiking enthusiasts. Trails of varying difficulty levels wind through the

Taurus Mountains, leading to breathtaking viewpoints, hidden waterfalls, and secluded mountain villages. One popular hiking destination is the Lycian Way, a long-distance trail that starts near Antalya and stretches along the coast, providing stunning vistas and a chance to connect with nature.

Rivers, Waterfalls, and Natural Reserves

Antalya is also home to several rivers and waterfalls, adding to its natural allure. The Duden Waterfalls, located northeast of the city center, cascade over rocky cliffs into the Mediterranean Sea, creating a mesmerizing spectacle. Another notable waterfall is Kursunlu Waterfall, nestled within a lush natural park, offering a peaceful retreat for visitors.

In addition to the waterfalls, there are various rivers that flow through the region. The Köprülü Canyon, carved by the Köprüçay River, is a popular spot for rafting and other water-based activities. The river's turquoise waters and stunning canyon walls create an exhilarating setting for adventure seekers.

Antalya is also home to several natural reserves and protected areas, such as the Olympos Beydaglari National Park and the Saklikent Gorge. These areas provide opportunities for hiking, wildlife observation, and experiencing the untouched beauty of nature.

Underwater Delights

Antalya's geographical features extend beneath the surface, making it a paradise for scuba diving and snorkeling enthusiasts. The crystal-clear waters of the Mediterranean Sea reveal a vibrant underwater world teeming with marine life, colorful coral reefs, and ancient shipwrecks. Diving sites such as the Sunken City of Kekova and the Antalya Aquarium offer unique experiences for underwater exploration.

The geographical features of Antalya, including its coastal landscapes, majestic mountains, waterfalls, and natural reserves, create a captivating setting for visitors. Whether you're seeking relaxation on the beaches, adventure in the mountains, or a journey into the underwater realm, Antalya's geography offers a wealth of opportunities to connect with nature and create lasting memories.

Climate and Best Time to Visit

Antalya enjoys a delightful Mediterranean climate characterized by hot, dry summers and mild, wet winters. The region experiences a pleasant year-round climate, making it an attractive destination for travelers. In this chapter, we will explore the climate of Antalya and provide recommendations for the best time to visit.

Climate Overview

Antalya's Mediterranean climate is influenced by its proximity to the sea and the surrounding Taurus Mountains. Summers in Antalya are hot and dry, with temperatures ranging from 30 to 35 degrees Celsius (86 to 95 degrees Fahrenheit). The city experiences long hours of sunshine, creating the perfect conditions for beach activities and outdoor exploration.

Winters in Antalya are mild and relatively wet. From December to February, temperatures range from 10 to 15 degrees Celsius (50 to 59 degrees Fahrenheit). Rainfall is more frequent during this period, but it is usually in the form of short, heavy showers. The mild winter climate allows visitors to explore historical sites and engage in various activities without extreme cold temperatures.

Best Time to Visit

The best time to visit Antalya largely depends on personal preferences and desired activities. Here are the seasons and factors to consider when planning your trip:

Spring (March to May): Spring is a pleasant time to visit Antalya as the weather begins to warm up. Temperatures range from 15 to 25 degrees Celsius (59 to 77 degrees Fahrenheit). The landscapes are lush and vibrant, making it ideal for outdoor activities and exploring historical sites. Spring is also a less crowded time, offering a more relaxed and authentic experience.

Summer (June to August): Summer is the peak tourist season in Antalya due to the warm and sunny weather. Temperatures range from 30 to 35 degrees Celsius (86 to 95 degrees Fahrenheit). It is the perfect time for beach lovers and water sports enthusiasts. However, keep in mind that popular tourist areas can be crowded during this period.

Autumn (September to November): Autumn brings pleasant temperatures ranging from 20 to 30 degrees Celsius (68 to 86 degrees Fahrenheit). The sea is still warm, and the weather is ideal for outdoor activities. Autumn is a great time to visit if you prefer to avoid the summer crowds while enjoying pleasant weather.

Winter (December to February): Antalya's mild winter climate makes it an appealing destination for winter escapes. While temperatures are cooler, ranging from 10 to 15 degrees Celsius (50 to 59 degrees Fahrenheit), Antalya still experiences milder weather compared to many other destinations. It is an excellent time for exploring historical sites, enjoying indoor activities, and experiencing local culture without crowds.

Special Considerations

It is important to note that Antalya can experience occasional heat waves during the summer months, with temperatures rising above 35 degrees Celsius (95 degrees Fahrenheit). It is advisable to stay hydrated, apply sunscreen, and seek shade during the hottest parts of the day if visiting during this time.

Additionally, if you plan to engage in water sports or scuba diving, the summer months provide the best conditions with warm water temperatures and excellent visibility.

Overall, the best time to visit Antalya depends on personal preferences. Spring and autumn offer pleasant weather and fewer crowds, making them popular choices for many travelers. Summer is perfect for beach activities and outdoor exploration, while winter provides a milder escape and a chance to explore historical sites without the peak tourist season.

By considering your interests and the climate conditions, you can choose the optimal time to visit Antalya and make the most of your experience.

II. Planning Your Trip

Travel Essentials

When planning your trip to Antalya, it's important to have a list of travel essentials to ensure a smooth and hassle-free experience. Here are some essential items and considerations to keep in mind:

Passport and Visa Requirements:

- Check the validity of your passport. Ensure it is valid for at least six months beyond your planned departure date. Depending on your nationality, you may need a visa to enter Turkey. Research and obtain the necessary visa in advance if required.

Travel Insurance:

- Consider purchasing travel insurance to protect yourself against unexpected events such as trip cancellations, medical emergencies, or lost baggage. Review the coverage details and policy terms to ensure it meets your needs and provides adequate protection during your trip.

Health Precautions:

- Consult with your healthcare provider or a travel clinic to check if any vaccinations or medications are recommended for your visit to Antalya. Ensure you have an adequate supply of any prescription medications you may need during your trip. It's also a good idea to pack a basic first-aid kit with essentials such as band-aids, pain relievers, and any personal medications.

Currency and Money Matters:

- Familiarize yourself with the local currency, which is the Turkish Lira (TRY). Check the current exchange rates and consider exchanging a small amount of currency before your departure. Locate ATMs in Antalya for easy access to cash, and inform your bank about your travel plans to avoid any issues with your credit or debit cards while abroad.

Travel Adapters and Chargers:

⬚ Antalya, like many countries, uses Type C and Type F electrical outlets with a voltage of 230V. Make sure to pack the appropriate travel adapters and chargers for your electronic devices to ensure you can stay connected and keep them powered during your trip.

Travel Documents and Copies:

⬚ Make digital and physical copies of important travel documents such as your passport, visa, travel insurance policy, and flight tickets. Keep the digital copies securely stored online or in cloud storage, and carry the physical copies separately from the originals.

Communication and Internet Access:

▢ Check with your mobile service provider about international roaming options or consider purchasing a local SIM card upon arrival in Antalya for cost-effective communication. Alternatively, take advantage of Wi-Fi availability in your accommodation or public areas to stay connected.

Travel Guides and Maps:

▢ Pack travel guides, and maps, or download relevant mobile applications to help navigate Antalya and plan your activities. These resources can provide valuable information on local attractions, transportation options, and recommendations for dining and sightseeing.

Travel Security:

⊠ Ensure the security of your belongings by using luggage locks and keeping valuables secure. Consider using a money belt or neck pouch to carry important documents and cash discreetly. Stay vigilant in crowded areas and beware of pickpockets.

Remember to double-check the specific requirements and recommendations for your country of origin before traveling to Antalya. Taking care of these travel essentials will help ensure a stress-free and enjoyable trip to this beautiful destination.

Visa Requirements and Entry Regulations

Visa requirements and entry regulations can vary depending on your nationality and the purpose and duration of your visit to Antalya. Here is some general information regarding visa requirements and entry regulations:

Visa Exemptions:

- Citizens of certain countries may be exempt from obtaining a visa for tourism or short-term visits. These exemptions can vary in terms of duration of stay and purpose of visit. It is essential to check if your country is eligible for visa exemption and the specific requirements that apply.

Electronic Visa (e-Visa):

- Turkey offers an e-Visa system for many nationalities, allowing travelers to apply for their visa online before their trip. The e-Visa is a simple and convenient way to obtain authorization to enter Turkey. Check the official website of the Turkish Ministry of Foreign Affairs for the list of eligible countries and the application process.

Visa on Arrival:

▢ Some nationalities have the option to obtain a visa upon arrival at Antalya Airport or other designated entry points. This facility is typically available for certain tourism and business purposes, and the duration of stay is limited. However, it is important to verify if you are eligible for a visa on arrival and the conditions that apply.

Visa Application at Consulate/Embassy:

▢ If your nationality is not eligible for visa exemption, e-Visa, or visa on arrival, you will need to apply for a visa at the nearest Turkish consulate or embassy in your country. Contact the consulate/embassy well in advance to gather the necessary information and initiate the visa application process.

Visa Requirements:

▫ When applying for a visa, you will generally need to submit certain documents, including a completed application form, passport-sized photos, a valid passport with sufficient remaining validity, proof of travel arrangements (such as flight bookings), proof of accommodation, travel insurance, and evidence of sufficient financial means to support your stay in Antalya.

It is crucial to review the specific visa requirements and regulations that apply to your nationality and purpose of visit. Visa requirements can change, so it is recommended to consult the official website of the Turkish Ministry of Foreign Affairs or contact the nearest Turkish consulate or embassy for the most up-to-date and accurate information regarding visa requirements and entry regulations for Antalya.

Transportation Options

When traveling to Antalya, there are various transportation options available to help you navigate within the city and explore the surrounding areas. Here are some transportation options to consider:

Getting to Antalya:

- **By Air:** Antalya has an international airport, Antalya Airport (AYT), which serves as a major transportation hub for the region. Many international airlines operate direct flights to Antalya from major cities around the world. Upon arrival, you can easily access the city center and other destinations using the transportation options available at the airport.

- **By Land:** If you prefer a land journey, you can reach Antalya by bus or car from other cities in Turkey or neighboring countries. Turkey has a well-developed bus network, and numerous bus companies offer routes to Antalya from various locations. Private car hire or organized tours are also options for those who prefer the flexibility and convenience of driving.

- **By Sea:** Antalya has a port, Antalya Cruise Port, which welcomes cruise ships and ferries. If you are arriving by sea, you can disembark at the port and explore Antalya and its surroundings using local transportation options.

Local Transportation:

- **Public Buses:** Antalya has a comprehensive network of public buses that operate within the city and connect to nearby areas. The buses are an affordable mode of transportation, and the routes cover popular tourist areas, beaches, and attractions. The Antalya Metropolitan Municipality operates the public bus system, and you can find information on routes, schedules, and fares on their official website or at bus stops.

- **Taxis:** Taxis are readily available in Antalya and provide a convenient way to get around the city. Taxis can be hailed on the street, found at designated taxi stands, or booked through taxi apps. Make sure the taxi meter is used, or negotiate the fare in advance to ensure a fair price. It is recommended to carry the address of your destination written in Turkish or have a map handy to communicate with the driver.

- **Car Rental:** Renting a car is an excellent option for those who prefer independence and flexibility in exploring Antalya and its surroundings. Several car rental companies have offices at Antalya Airport and within the city. Make sure to familiarize yourself with local traffic rules and regulations, and carry the necessary documents, including a valid driver's license and insurance, when driving in Antalya.

- **Bicycle Rental:** Antalya has an increasing number of bike rental services, offering a fun and eco-friendly way to explore the city. Some areas have dedicated bike lanes and paths, making it convenient to cycle around popular sites. Remember to wear a helmet and follow traffic rules when riding a bike in Antalya.

- **Walking:** Antalya's city center, particularly the historic Kaleici district, is best explored on foot. The narrow streets, charming alleys, and historical landmarks are easily accessible by walking. Walking allows you to soak in the ambiance, discover hidden gems, and enjoy the local culture at your own pace.

Day Trips and Excursions:

- ☒ **Organized Tours:** If you wish to visit popular attractions and landmarks outside of Antalya, organized tours are available. These tours typically include transportation, a guide, and visits to key sites such as ancient cities, natural wonders, or cultural destinations. You can find a variety of tours through local tour operators, travel agencies, or online platforms.

- ☒ **Private Transfers:** For a more personalized experience, private transfers can be arranged for day trips or excursions. Private drivers or tour guides can provide transportation and tailor the itinerary according to your preferences and interests.

Consider your budget, preferences, and the specific locations you plan to visit when choosing your transportation options in Antalya. Each option offers its own advantages, so select the mode of transportation that suits your needs and allows you to make the most of your time exploring this captivating city.

Accommodation Choices

Antalya offers a wide range of accommodation options to suit different budgets, preferences, and travel styles. Whether you're seeking luxury, convenience, or a more budget-friendly stay, you'll find a variety of choices throughout the city. Here are some popular accommodation options in Antalya:

Luxury Resorts and Hotels:

- ⬚ Antalya is known for its luxurious resorts and hotels that provide top-notch amenities, stunning views, and exceptional service. These establishments often feature multiple swimming pools, spa facilities, fine dining restaurants, and private beach access. If you're looking for a pampering and indulgent experience, luxury resorts and hotels in areas like Lara and Belek are ideal options.

Boutique Hotels:

⬚ For a more intimate and personalized experience, boutique hotels in Antalya offer a unique charm and character. These smaller, independently owned hotels often have distinctive decor, stylish interiors, and attentive service. Boutique hotels are scattered throughout the city, particularly in the historic Kaleici district, allowing you to immerse yourself in the local ambiance.

All-Inclusive Resorts:

⬚ Antalya is home to numerous all-inclusive resorts that provide a convenient and hassle-free vacation experience. These resorts typically offer accommodations, meals, drinks, and various amenities within the property. All-inclusive resorts can be found along the coast, particularly in areas like Lara, and are popular among families and travelers seeking a comprehensive package.

Budget Accommodations:

⬛ Travelers on a tighter budget will find several budget-friendly accommodation options in Antalya. Hostels and guesthouses provide affordable dormitory or private room options with shared facilities. These budget accommodations are often located in the city center or near popular tourist areas, making them convenient for exploring Antalya on a limited budget.

Vacation Rentals:

⬛ Vacation rentals, such as apartments or villas, are increasingly popular in Antalya. They provide a home-away-from-home experience, with the convenience of having a kitchen, living space, and additional amenities. Vacation rentals are suitable for families or groups of friends who prefer a more independent and spacious accommodation option.

Location Considerations:

 When choosing your accommodation in Antalya, consider the location based on your preferences and planned activities. The city center, Kaleici, is a popular choice for its historical charm, narrow streets, and proximity to cultural attractions. If you prefer a beachfront stay, areas like Lara, Konyaalti, or Belek offer a range of accommodations with direct access to the beautiful Mediterranean coast.

Online Booking Platforms:

- Utilize online booking platforms to search and compare accommodation options in Antalya. Websites and apps such as Booking.com, Airbnb, or Expedia offer a wide selection of properties, allowing you to filter by price, location, and amenities. Read reviews from previous guests to get an idea of the quality and service of each establishment.

Reservation Tips:

- Once you have chosen your desired accommodation, it is advisable to make a reservation in advance, especially during peak travel seasons. This ensures availability and often provides the opportunity to secure better rates or special offers. Contact the accommodation directly or use online booking platforms to complete your reservation.

Consider your preferences, budget, and the purpose of your visit when selecting your accommodation in Antalya. Whether you opt for luxury, boutique, budget, or alternative options, Antalya offers a range of choices to suit every traveler's needs.

Budgeting and Currency

When planning your trip to Antalya, it's essential to consider your budget and understand the local currency to ensure a smooth and enjoyable experience. Here are some important factors to consider regarding budgeting and currency in Antalya:

Trip Budget:

- Set a realistic budget for your trip to Antalya. Consider your accommodation, transportation, meals, activities, souvenirs, and any additional expenses you may incur during your stay. Research average costs for meals, attractions, and transportation to help estimate your daily expenses.

Currency in Antalya:

⬚ The official currency in Antalya, as well as throughout Turkey, is the Turkish Lira (TRY). Familiarize yourself with the currency and its denominations. It's advisable to carry a mix of cash and have a debit/credit card for convenience.

Currency Exchange:

⬚ Locate exchange offices or ATMs in Antalya to exchange your currency for Turkish Lira. Major airports, city centers, and tourist areas generally have currency exchange facilities. Compare exchange rates and fees to ensure you get a fair deal. It's a good idea to have some local currency on hand for smaller establishments that may not accept cards.

Credit/Debit Cards and ATMs:

 Credit and debit cards are widely accepted in most hotels, restaurants, and larger establishments in Antalya. Visa and Mastercard are the most commonly accepted cards, followed by American Express and Diners Club. Inform your bank or credit card company about your travel plans to avoid any issues with card transactions. Additionally, locate ATMs in Antalya to withdraw cash as needed. Be mindful of any fees or foreign transaction charges imposed by your bank.

Tipping and Service Charges:

 Tipping is a common practice in Antalya. In restaurants, it is customary to leave a 10-15% tip for good service. However, check if a service charge is already included in the bill before adding an additional tip. For taxi rides, rounding up the fare or leaving a small tip is appreciated. It is also customary to tip hotel staff, tour guides, and other service providers if you are satisfied with their services.

Bargaining and Negotiating Prices:

 Bargaining or negotiating prices is common in certain situations, such as in markets, bazaars, or when purchasing goods or services from street vendors. Use your judgment and negotiate respectfully. Keep in mind that bargaining may not be appropriate or accepted in all situations, such as in established shops or restaurants.

Safety and Security:

 Exercise caution when handling money and keep your belongings secure. Avoid displaying large sums of cash in public and use hotel safes or other secure storage options for valuables. Be cautious of potential scams or pickpocketing in crowded areas, and keep an eye on your belongings at all times.

Emergency Funds:

⬚ It's always wise to have emergency funds or a backup payment method available in case of unforeseen circumstances. Carry a small amount of local currency and keep a copy of important financial information, such as card numbers and emergency contact details, in a safe place.

By considering these budgeting and currency tips, you can manage your finances effectively and have a worry-free experience in Antalya. Plan your budget in advance, exchange currency at reputable locations, and keep track of your expenses to make the most of your trip.

III. Exploring Antalya City

Antalya City, the vibrant hub of the Antalya province, offers a captivating blend of history, culture, and natural beauty. Located on the southwestern coast of Turkey, this bustling city is renowned for its stunning beaches, ancient sites, and lively atmosphere. In this chapter, we will explore the various facets of Antalya City and provide recommendations for exploring its many attractions.

Old Town (Kaleici)

Kaleici, also known as the Old Town, is a captivating neighborhood located within the heart of Antalya City. This historical district is a treasure trove of narrow cobblestone streets, charming Ottoman-era houses, ancient Roman walls, and remnants of past civilizations. Exploring Kaleici is like stepping back in time, offering a glimpse into the rich history and cultural heritage of Antalya. Here's what you can discover in the Old Town:

Hadrian's Gate:

- ☒ One of the most iconic landmarks in Antalya, Hadrian's Gate is a beautifully preserved Roman triumphal arch that was built in 130 AD to honor the visit of Emperor Hadrian. This majestic gate marks the entrance to the old city and is adorned with intricate carvings and detailed reliefs. Passing through this grand archway is like stepping into a world of ancient wonders.

Kesik Minaret (Broken Minaret):

- ☒ The Kesik Minaret, also known as the Broken Minaret, is a remarkable structure that dates back to the 2nd century AD. Originally part of a Byzantine church, it later became a mosque. Today, the minaret stands as a symbol of the city's diverse architectural history. Though the church was destroyed in an earthquake, the minaret survived and serves as a reminder of Antalya's past.

Historical Houses:

⬚ Walking through the narrow streets of Kaleici, you'll come across beautifully preserved Ottoman-era houses with their distinct architecture and wooden balconies. Some of these houses have been converted into boutique hotels, cafes, and shops, while others still serve as private residences. Marvel at the traditional architectural details and imagine the lives of those who once inhabited these historical homes.

Hidirlik Tower:

⬚ Situated near the ancient port of Antalya, Hidirlik Tower is a historical structure believed to have been constructed during the Roman period. This cylindrical tower offers panoramic views of the city and the Mediterranean Sea. Climb to the top to enjoy a breathtaking vista and capture memorable photographs of the surrounding landscapes.

Historical Sites and Ruins:

⬛ Within Kaleici, you'll find numerous historical sites and ruins that reflect the city's rich past. Explore the remains of ancient Roman walls, visit the Yivli Minare (Fluted Minaret) and the nearby Alaeddin Mosque, or discover the remnants of ancient buildings scattered throughout the neighborhood. These archaeological treasures provide a fascinating insight into Antalya's storied history.

Shops, Cafes, and Restaurants:

⬛ Kaleici is not just a haven for history enthusiasts; it's also a vibrant hub for shopping, dining, and relaxation. Wander through the maze-like streets lined with boutique shops selling traditional crafts, jewelry, carpets, and souvenirs. Pause for a cup of Turkish tea or coffee at a charming café, and savor the flavors of local cuisine in the traditional restaurants that dot the neighborhood.

Nightlife in Kaleici:

▢ As the sun sets, Kaleici takes on a different ambiance, with its narrow streets illuminated by soft lights. The district offers a cozy and intimate setting for evening strolls, romantic dinners, and vibrant nightlife. Enjoy live music performances, indulge in a glass of Turkish wine at a rooftop bar, or simply immerse yourself in the enchanting atmosphere of the Old Town after dark.

Kaleici is a captivating blend of history, culture, and charm. It invites visitors to explore its winding streets, admire its architectural wonders, and embrace the essence of Antalya's past. Immerse yourself in the rich heritage of the Old Town and create lasting memories as you uncover its hidden treasures.

Antalya Marina

The Antalya Marina is a vibrant waterfront area that offers a picturesque setting and a multitude of activities for visitors to enjoy. Located near the city center, the marina serves as a hub for boats, yachts, and seaside entertainment. Here's what you can discover and experience at the Antalya Marina:

Scenic Promenade:

- The marina boasts a scenic promenade that stretches along the waterfront, offering a delightful place to take a leisurely stroll.

Enjoy the refreshing sea breeze, admire the stunning views of the Mediterranean Sea, and soak up the lively atmosphere of the marina.

Yacht and Boat Watching:

◻ The Antalya Marina is home to an array of boats and yachts of different sizes and designs. Take a moment to marvel at the impressive vessels, from luxury yachts to traditional wooden sailboats. Watch as they glide through the crystal-clear waters, adding to the allure of the marina.

Waterside Dining:

◻ Numerous restaurants and cafes line the marina, providing a wonderful opportunity to indulge in delicious cuisine while enjoying the waterfront views. Treat yourself to a meal of fresh seafood, Turkish specialties, or international dishes, all while relishing the charming ambiance of the marina.

Sunset Views:

 ⊠ The Antalya Marina offers a breathtaking vantage point to witness stunning sunsets over the Mediterranean Sea. As the sun dips below the horizon, the sky is painted with vibrant hues of orange, pink, and purple, creating a mesmerizing backdrop for a romantic evening.

Boat Tours and Excursions:

 ⊠ The marina serves as a starting point for various boat tours and excursions that allow you to explore the beautiful coastline and nearby attractions. Hop aboard a boat and cruise along the turquoise waters, discovering hidden coves, secluded beaches, and charming coastal villages. Some tours also offer opportunities for swimming, snorkeling, or diving in crystal-clear waters.

Fishing Opportunities:

 Fishing enthusiasts can try their hand at angling in the waters around the marina. Join a fishing charter or rent your own equipment, and cast your line to catch local fish species. Whether you're an experienced angler or a beginner, the marina provides a scenic and relaxing environment for fishing.

Shopping and Souvenirs

 The marina area features several shops and boutiques where you can browse for souvenirs, beachwear, accessories, and nautical-themed items. Take a leisurely shopping stroll and pick up a memento to remember your time in Antalya or find a unique gift for someone special.

Vibrant Nightlife:

- As evening falls, the Antalya Marina comes alive with its vibrant nightlife scene. Numerous bars and pubs offer a lively atmosphere, where you can enjoy live music, dance to the tunes of DJs, or simply unwind with a cocktail while overlooking the marina. The combination of the sparkling sea, energetic music, and friendly ambiance set the stage for a memorable evening.

The Antalya Marina is a captivating destination that combines natural beauty, waterfront dining, recreational activities, and a lively atmosphere. Whether you're looking to enjoy a leisurely stroll, embark on a boat tour, or savor delicious cuisine with a view, the marina offers a delightful experience for visitors of all ages.

Hadrian's Gate

Hadrian's Gate, also known as Hadrianus Kapısı in Turkish, is a magnificent Roman triumphal arch that stands as one of the most iconic landmarks in Antalya. This impressive structure dates back to the 2nd century AD and was built to honor the visit of Emperor Hadrian to the city. Here's what you can discover about Hadrian's Gate:

Historical Significance:

- Hadrian's Gate holds great historical significance as it marks the entrance to the ancient city of Antalya (then called Attaleia). The gate was built during the reign of Emperor Hadrian in 130 AD, serving as a symbol of the city's connection to the Roman Empire.

Architectural Beauty:

- The gate showcases exquisite Roman architectural style and craftsmanship.

It consists of three arched entrances with detailed decorations and intricate reliefs. The central arch is larger and more ornate, while the smaller side arches were used for pedestrian access.

Decorative Elements:

- The façade of Hadrian's Gate is adorned with intricate carvings and reliefs. The reliefs depict mythological scenes, including Emperor Hadrian's journey and various gods and goddesses. The decorative elements showcase the artistic and cultural influences of the Roman period.

Marvelous Symmetry:

- The design of Hadrian's Gate exhibits remarkable symmetry and proportion. The architectural details, including columns, pilasters, and ornamental motifs, create a visually striking ensemble. The gate's structure stands as a testament to the engineering and architectural achievements of the Roman Empire.

Integration with the City:

- Hadrian's Gate seamlessly blends with the surrounding cityscape, as it serves as an entry point to the historic Kaleici (Old Town) district. Passing through the gate takes you from the modern city to the enchanting realm of narrow streets, Ottoman-era houses, and ancient ruins.

Photography and Views:

- Hadrian's Gate offers an excellent photo opportunity for capturing the grandeur of ancient Roman architecture. Photographers will appreciate the juxtaposition of the gate with the modern city backdrop. Climbing to the top of the gate provides panoramic views of the surrounding area, allowing you to

capture   breathtaking   vistas   of
Antalya.

Accessibility and Proximity:

⬚   Hadrian's Gate is conveniently located near the city center, making it easily accessible on foot or by public transportation. It serves as a gateway to explore the historical Kaleici district, with its labyrinthine streets, charming shops, and authentic Turkish cafes and restaurants.

Visiting Hadrian's Gate allows you to step back in time and witness the grandeur of the Roman Empire. It's architectural splendor and historical significance make it a must-see attraction for travelers exploring the captivating city of Antalya.

Antalya Museum

The Antalya Museum, also known as the Antalya Archaeological Museum, is a treasure trove of artifacts that offers a fascinating journey through the history and cultural heritage of the Antalya region. Located in Konyaalti, just a short distance from the city center, this renowned museum is a must-visit destination for history enthusiasts and those seeking a deeper understanding of the region's rich past. Here's what you can discover at the Antalya Museum:

Extensive Artifact Collection:

- The museum boasts an extensive collection of artifacts that span various periods and civilizations, dating back thousands of years. The exhibits showcase archaeological finds from the Paleolithic, Neolithic, Hellenistic, Roman, Byzantine, and Ottoman eras. Marvel at the intricate sculptures, detailed mosaics, ancient coins, pottery, jewelry, and other objects that provide insights into the lives of past civilizations.

Hall of Regional Excavations:

⊠ The museum's Hall of Regional Excavations focuses specifically on the archaeological discoveries made in the Antalya region. Explore the exhibits that highlight the ancient cities, ancient theaters, tombs, and other archaeological sites found within the vicinity of Antalya. Gain a deeper understanding of the historical significance of the region and the civilizations that once thrived there.

Themed Exhibition Halls:

⊠ The Antalya Museum features themed exhibition halls that focus on specific aspects of history and culture. Explore halls dedicated to ancient cities, mythological stories, Roman emperors, sarcophagi, and more. Each hall provides a curated experience that showcases the artifacts and their historical context, offering a comprehensive view of the region's past.

Perge and Aspendos Collections:

⊠ The museum houses remarkable collections from two prominent ancient cities in the Antalya region: Perge and Aspendos. These collections showcase sculptures, reliefs, inscriptions, and other artifacts that were excavated from the archaeological sites of these ancient cities. Gain insight into the artistic achievements and cultural practices of these ancient civilizations.

Conservation Laboratory:

⊠ The Antalya Museum is also home to a conservation laboratory where ongoing preservation efforts take place. Witness firsthand the meticulous work undertaken to restore and conserve ancient artifacts, ensuring their longevity and preservation for future generations.

Educational Programs and Workshops:

⊠ The museum offers educational programs and workshops for visitors of all ages. Engage in guided tours to learn more about the exhibits, attend lectures and presentations on archaeological topics, or participate in hands-on workshops that allow you to experience ancient crafts and techniques.

Outdoor Garden:

⊠ The museum features an outdoor garden area where you can take a leisurely stroll and enjoy the tranquil surroundings. Admire the archaeological artifacts displayed in the garden, including sarcophagi, statues, and architectural fragments. The garden offers a serene escape and a chance to appreciate the fusion of history and nature.

A visit to the Antalya Museum provides a unique opportunity to delve into the region's rich history and witness the remarkable artifacts that have been unearthed over centuries. Immerse yourself in the fascinating stories of ancient civilizations and gain a deeper appreciation for the cultural heritage of Antalya and its surroundings.

Yivliminare Mosque

The Yivliminare Mosque, also known as the Fluted Minaret Mosque or Alaaddin Mosque, is a remarkable architectural gem located in the heart of Antalya. This iconic mosque stands as a testament to the city's rich history and showcases the beauty of Seljuk architecture. Here's what you can discover about the Yivliminare Mosque:

Historical Significance:

◆ The Yivliminare Mosque dates back to the 13th century, built during the reign of Sultan Alaaddin Keykubad I, the Seljuk ruler of the time. It holds great historical and cultural importance as one of the oldest mosques in Antalya and a symbol of the city's connection to the Seljuk Empire.

Architectural Marvel:

◆ The mosque's most distinctive feature is its fluted minaret, which gives the mosque its name. The minaret stands tall at approximately 38 meters (124 feet) and is adorned with intricate brickwork and decorative patterns. Its elegant and slender design captivates visitors and showcases the ingenuity of Seljuk architecture.

Seljuk Influence:

- The Yivliminare Mosque exemplifies the Seljuk architectural style, characterized by geometric patterns, ornamental motifs, and intricate stonework. The mosque showcases the expertise of Seljuk craftsmen in blending Islamic and local Anatolian architectural traditions.

Interior Beauty:

- Step inside the mosque to admire its interior beauty. The prayer hall features a spacious and tranquil atmosphere adorned with elegant calligraphy, colorful stained glass windows, and intricately painted ceilings. The subdued lighting creates a serene ambiance that invites visitors to reflect and appreciate the spiritual significance of the space.

Courtyard and Surroundings:

⬚ The mosque is surrounded by a peaceful courtyard where visitors can find a sense of tranquility. Take a moment to relax in the courtyard and admire the architectural elements that adorn the mosque's exterior, including the ornate entrance gate and the exquisite details of the minaret.

Preservation and Restoration:

⬚ Over the years, the Yivliminare Mosque has undergone several preservation and restoration efforts to ensure its structural integrity and historical authenticity. The meticulous restoration work has maintained the mosque's original features and ensured its continued existence as a prominent cultural and religious site.

Cultural Significance:

- ⬚ The Yivliminare Mosque continues to serve as an active place of worship for the local Muslim community, making it a living testament to Antalya's cultural and religious heritage. Visitors have the opportunity to observe the practices and rituals of daily prayers, further enhancing their understanding of the mosque's role in contemporary Antalya.

Visiting the Yivliminare Mosque allows you to appreciate the architectural splendor and cultural significance of this historic site. The mosque's intricate details, Seljuk influences, and serene atmosphere combine to create an awe-inspiring experience that showcases the beauty of Antalya's architectural heritage.

Ataturk House Museum

The Ataturk House Museum, also known as Ataturk Evi Müzesi in Turkish, is a significant historical site in Antalya that offers a glimpse into the life and legacy of Mustafa Kemal Ataturk, the founder of modern Turkey. Located in the historic Kaleici district, this museum was once the residence of Ataturk during his visits to Antalya. Here's what you can discover at the Ataturk House Museum:

Historical Significance:

- The Ataturk House Museum holds great historical significance as it was the residence of Mustafa Kemal Ataturk, the founder and first president of the Republic of Turkey. Ataturk visited the house on his trips to Antalya in the 1930s, and it has been preserved as a museum to honor his memory.

Ataturk's Visits:

⬚ Mustafa Kemal Ataturk, revered as the father of modern Turkey, stayed in this house during his visits to Antalya. The museum provides a glimpse into Ataturk's life and offers insight into his connection with the city.

Authenticity and Preservation:

⬚ The Ataturk House Museum has been carefully preserved to maintain its original appearance and authenticity. The rooms have been furnished and decorated to reflect the time period when Ataturk stayed in the house, allowing visitors to step back in time and experience the ambiance of his visits.

Ataturk Memorabilia:

⬚ Inside the museum, you'll find a collection of personal belongings, photographs, and memorabilia

74

associated with Ataturk. These items provide a deeper understanding of his life, achievements, and the impact he had on the establishment of modern Turkey.

Architecture and Design:

 The Ataturk House Museum showcases traditional Ottoman architecture and design elements. From the architectural details of the building to the interior furnishings, visitors can appreciate the historical aesthetics and cultural influences that shaped the house.

Peaceful Garden:

 The museum includes a tranquil garden area where visitors can relax and enjoy the serene atmosphere. Take a moment to stroll through the garden, surrounded by lush greenery and blooming flowers, and reflect on

Ataturk's legacy and his contributions to the nation.

Educational Significance:

- The Ataturk House Museum serves as an educational site that sheds light on Turkey's modern history. Guided tours and informative displays provide valuable insights into Ataturk's life, his vision for the country, and the progress made during his presidency.

Visiting the Ataturk House Museum offers a unique opportunity to step into the world of Mustafa Kemal Ataturk and gain a deeper appreciation for his role in shaping Turkey's history. The museum allows visitors to understand the personal side of Ataturk and his connection to Antalya, making it a significant cultural and historical destination within the city.

IV. Beaches and Coastal Attractions in Antalya

Antalya are renowned for their stunning coastline and pristine beaches that offer a paradise-like setting for relaxation and water-based activities. Whether you're seeking a tranquil escape or an adventurous seaside experience, here are some of the top beaches and coastal attractions in Antalya:

Konyaalti Beach:

- Located west of the city center, Konyaalti Beach is a popular stretch of golden sand that extends for several kilometers along the coast. With its crystal-clear turquoise waters and breathtaking mountain views, it offers a picturesque setting for sunbathing, swimming, and enjoying a leisurely stroll along the promenade.

Lara Beach:

⬚ Situated to the east of Antalya, Lara Beach is known for its expansive stretch of soft, sandy coastline. The beach is home to numerous luxurious resorts, each with its own private section of the beach. Enjoy the amenities offered by the resorts, indulge in water sports, or simply bask in the sun while admiring the stunning surroundings.

Kaputas Beach:

⬚ Located between Kas and Kalkan, Kaputas Beach is a hidden gem tucked away at the base of a dramatic gorge. Accessible via a steep staircase, this secluded beach is renowned for its turquoise waters, rocky cliffs, and pristine natural beauty. Spend a day sunbathing, swimming, and snorkeling in crystal-clear waters that are perfect for marine exploration.

Phaselis Beach:

- Situated within the ancient city of Phaselis, this beach offers a unique combination of historical ruins and natural beauty. Surrounded by pine forests and boasting crystal-clear waters, Phaselis Beach is an idyllic spot for sunbathing and swimming. Take a leisurely walk through the ancient ruins of Phaselis, located just a stone's throw away from the beach.

Cirali Beach:

⬚ Nestled in a tranquil bay at the foot of the majestic Mount Olympos, Cirali Beach is known for its unspoiled beauty and pristine environment. This protected beach is a nesting site for loggerhead sea turtles, adding to its ecological significance. Enjoy the peaceful ambiance, take a refreshing swim, and witness the captivating natural beauty that surrounds the area.

Olympos Beach:

⬚ Adjacent to Cirali Beach, Olympos Beach offers a unique blend of history and natural splendor. Explore the ancient ruins of Olympos, including the impressive Olympos Ruins and the Chimera flames, before relaxing on the pebbly beach. This laid-back beach is a perfect spot for unwinding and enjoying the serene coastal atmosphere.

Patara Beach:

◌ Located further west of Antalya, Patara Beach is a breathtaking stretch of coastline renowned for its long, sandy beach and pristine natural surroundings. As one of the longest beaches in Turkey, it offers ample space for sunbathing and relaxation. Discover the nearby ancient ruins of Patara, including the well-preserved Roman amphitheater, to complete your coastal adventure.

Alanya Beaches:

◌ Just outside of Antalya, the coastal town of Alanya boasts several beautiful beaches that attract visitors from near and far. Cleopatra Beach, with its fine golden sand, is a popular choice, while Keykubat Beach offers a family-friendly atmosphere with its shallow waters and water sports options. Explore the caves and cliffs that dot the coastline, adding an element of adventure to your beach visit.

Whether you're looking for tranquility, water sports, or a blend of history and natural beauty, the beaches and coastal attractions of Antalya offer something for everyone. Embrace the sun, sand, and sea as you create unforgettable memories in these stunning coastal destinations.

V. Natural Wonders and Outdoor Adventures in Antalya

Antalya is a region blessed with remarkable natural beauty and a diverse landscape that beckons outdoor enthusiasts and nature lovers. From soaring mountains to picturesque waterfalls, here are some of the natural wonders and outdoor adventures to explore in Antalya:

Mount Tahtali:

- Rising majestically above the coastline, Mount Tahtali offers breathtaking panoramic views of the region. Embark on a cable car ride to the summit, where you'll be rewarded with stunning vistas of the Mediterranean Sea, the Taurus Mountains, and the surrounding landscapes. For the adventurous, hiking trails provide an opportunity to conquer the mountain on foot.

Duden Waterfalls:

- The Duden Waterfalls, located just a short distance from the city center, are a spectacular sight to behold. The Lower Duden Waterfalls cascade directly into the Mediterranean Sea, creating a mesmerizing display of natural beauty. Take a boat tour to witness the falls up close, or enjoy a leisurely stroll along the pathway that runs alongside the rushing waters.

Saklikent Gorge:

- Venture to the Saklikent Gorge, a natural wonder nestled in the Taurus Mountains. This awe-inspiring gorge offers a unique hiking and adventure experience. Wade through the icy waters, hike along the gorge walls or try canyoning and rafting for an adrenaline-pumping adventure. The breathtaking scenery and refreshing atmosphere make this a must-visit destination for outdoor enthusiasts.

Kursunlu Waterfall:

- Located in a lush nature park, the Kursunlu Waterfall is a serene oasis of tranquility. Surrounded by dense forests and rich flora, the waterfall cascades over the rocks, creating a picturesque setting. Take a leisurely walk along the nature trails, breathe in the fresh air, and appreciate the beauty of this hidden gem.

Termessos Archaeological Site:

⊠ Explore the ancient ruins of Termessos, an archaeological site nestled in the rugged Taurus Mountains. This well-preserved city offers a unique glimpse into the past, surrounded by stunning natural landscapes. Hike through the rocky terrain, admire the ancient ruins, and take in the panoramic views from the hilltop theater.

Olympos Cable Car and Beydaglari National Park:

⊠ Take a cable car ride in Beydaglari National Park, ascending to the heights of the Taurus Mountains. Enjoy the breathtaking views as you glide above the rugged terrain, dense forests, and deep valleys. The national park offers opportunities for hiking, picnicking, and immersing yourself in the pristine natural surroundings.

Boat Tours and Blue Cruise:

- Embark on a boat tour or a Blue Cruise to explore the stunning coastline of Antalya. Sail along the turquoise waters, stopping at hidden coves, secluded beaches, and charming islands. Swim in crystal-clear bays, snorkel in vibrant underwater worlds, and relax on the deck, soaking in the sun and sea breeze.

Jeep Safari and Quad Biking:

- Experience an exhilarating off-road adventure by joining a jeep safari or quad biking tour. Explore rugged terrains, traverse through pine forests, and navigate off-the-beaten-path trails. These adrenaline-filled excursions allow you to discover the natural wonders of Antalya's hinterland while enjoying an exciting outdoor adventure.

Antalya's natural wonders and outdoor adventures offer a wealth of opportunities to connect with nature and experience the thrill of exploration. Whether you seek breathtaking views, peaceful hikes, adrenaline-pumping activities, or serene natural oases, Antalya's diverse landscapes will leave you in awe of the region's remarkable beauty.

Day Trips and Excursions from Antalya

While Antalya itself offers a wealth of attractions and experiences, the region surrounding the city is also dotted with fascinating destinations and hidden gems. Embark on day trips and excursions to explore the diverse landscapes, ancient ruins, and charming towns nearby. Here are some recommended day trips and excursions from Antalya:

Side:

◻ Venture east of Antalya to the ancient city of Side, known for its well-preserved Roman ruins and stunning coastal setting. Explore the grand Temple of Apollo, the impressive Theater, and the ancient Agora. Stroll through the charming streets lined with shops, cafes, and restaurants, and relax on Side's beautiful beaches.

Perge:

◻ Visit the ancient city of Perge, located just a short drive from Antalya. Marvel at the well-preserved ruins of this once-prosperous city, including the impressive Roman Theater, the monumental gate, and the ancient stadium. Immerse yourself in the rich history as you wander through the colonnaded streets and admire the intricate details of the ancient structures.

Aspendos:

- Discover the ancient city of Aspendos, renowned for its magnificent Roman Theater, one of the best-preserved theaters from antiquity. Marvel at the remarkable architecture and acoustics of this ancient masterpiece. Explore the ruins of Aspendos, including the Agora and the impressive aqueduct that once supplied water to the city.

Demre and Myra:

- Journey to the coastal town of Demre to explore the fascinating Lycian ruins of Myra. Admire the beautifully carved rock-cut tombs and the well-preserved Roman theater. Visit the Church of St. Nicholas, the resting place of the legendary figure of Santa Claus. Take a boat tour to the nearby island of Kekova to witness the fascinating underwater ruins.

Pamukkale and Hierapolis:

    ▯   Embark on a mesmerizing journey to Pamukkale, a UNESCO World Heritage Site famous for its cascading travertine terraces and mineral-rich thermal waters. Explore the ancient city of Hierapolis, with its well-preserved ruins, including the ancient theater, the Roman bathhouses, and the Necropolis. Relax in the thermal pools of Pamukkale for a truly rejuvenating experience.

Termessos and Karain Cave:

    ▯   Head into the rugged Taurus Mountains to explore the ancient city of Termessos, perched high on a mountainside. Marvel at the well-preserved ruins, including the theater, the agora, and the impressive city walls. Afterward, visit Karain Cave, one of the oldest inhabited caves in Turkey, where fascinating archaeological discoveries have been made.

Taurus Mountains Jeep Safari:

- ⊠ Embark on a thrilling jeep safari adventure into the scenic Taurus Mountains. Traverse off-road trails, discover hidden villages and enjoy panoramic views of the surrounding landscapes. Experience the local culture, taste traditional cuisine, and connect with the natural beauty of the mountainous region.

Boat Trip to Kekova and Simena:

- ⊠ Set sail on a boat trip to the picturesque island of Kekova and the charming village of Simena. Cruise along the turquoise waters, admiring the sunken ruins of Kekova, and snorkel in the crystal-clear bays. Explore the ancient castle in Simena, stroll through its quaint streets, and savor delicious seafood in local waterfront restaurants.

These day trips and excursions from Antalya offer a wealth of opportunities to explore ancient history, natural wonders, and charming towns. Whether you're fascinated by archaeology, drawn to scenic landscapes, or seeking cultural immersion, these nearby destinations will enrich your Antalya experience and create lasting memories.

VI. Day Trips and Excursions from Antalya

While Antalya itself offers a wealth of attractions and experiences, the region surrounding the city is also dotted with fascinating destinations and hidden gems. Embark on day trips and excursions to explore the diverse landscapes, ancient ruins, and charming towns nearby. Here are some recommended day trips and excursions from Antalya:

Side:

- ⊠ Venture east of Antalya to the ancient city of Side, known for its well-preserved Roman ruins and stunning coastal setting. Explore the grand Temple of Apollo, the impressive Theater, and the ancient Agora. Stroll through the charming streets lined with shops, cafes, and restaurants, and relax on Side's beautiful beaches.

Perge:

- ⬚ Visit the ancient city of Perge, located just a short drive from Antalya. Marvel at the well-preserved ruins of this once-prosperous city, including the impressive Roman Theater, the monumental gate, and the ancient stadium. Immerse yourself in the rich history as you wander through the colonnaded streets and admire the intricate details of the ancient structures.

Aspendos:

- ⬚ Discover the ancient city of Aspendos, renowned for its magnificent Roman Theater, one of the best-preserved theaters from antiquity. Marvel at the remarkable architecture and acoustics of this ancient masterpiece. Explore the ruins of Aspendos, including the Agora and the impressive aqueduct that once supplied water to the city.

Demre and Myra:

🔲 Journey to the coastal town of Demre to explore the fascinating Lycian ruins of Myra. Admire the beautifully carved rock-cut tombs and the well-preserved Roman theater. Visit the Church of St. Nicholas, the resting place of the legendary figure of Santa Claus. Take a boat tour to the nearby island of Kekova to witness the fascinating underwater ruins.

Pamukkale and Hierapolis:

🔲 Embark on a mesmerizing journey to Pamukkale, a UNESCO World Heritage Site famous for its cascading travertine terraces and mineral-rich thermal waters. Explore the ancient city of Hierapolis, with its well-preserved ruins, including the ancient theater, the Roman bathhouses, and the Necropolis. Relax in the thermal pools of Pamukkale for a truly rejuvenating experience.

Termessos and Karain Cave:

- Head into the rugged Taurus Mountains to explore the ancient city of Termessos, perched high on a mountainside. Marvel at the well-preserved ruins, including the theater, the agora, and the impressive city walls. Afterward, visit Karain Cave, one of the oldest inhabited caves in Turkey, where fascinating archaeological discoveries have been made.

Taurus Mountains Jeep Safari:

- Embark on a thrilling jeep safari adventure into the scenic Taurus Mountains. Traverse off-road trails, discover hidden villages, and enjoy panoramic views of the surrounding landscapes. Experience the local culture, taste traditional cuisine, and connect with the natural beauty of the mountainous region.

Boat Trip to Kekova and Simena:

 Set sail on a boat trip to the picturesque island of Kekova and the charming village of Simena. Cruise along the turquoise waters, admiring the sunken ruins of Kekova, and snorkel in the crystal-clear bays. Explore the ancient castle in Simena, stroll through its quaint streets, and savor delicious seafood in local waterfront restaurants.

These day trips and excursions from Antalya offer a wealth of opportunities to explore ancient history, natural wonders, and charming towns. Whether you're fascinated by archaeology, drawn to scenic landscapes, or seeking cultural immersion, these nearby destinations will enrich your Antalya experience and create lasting memories.

VII. Turkish Cuisine and Dining

Popular Local Dishes in Antalya

Antalya boasts a vibrant culinary scene that combines traditional Turkish flavors with Mediterranean influences. Here are some popular local dishes you should try during your visit:

Piyaz:

- Piyaz is a traditional Turkish salad made with white beans, onions, tomatoes, and parsley, dressed with olive oil, lemon juice, and spices. It is a refreshing and flavorful starter that pairs well with grilled meats or as a side dish.

Tantuni:

- Tantuni is a popular street food dish in Antalya. It consists of thinly sliced and sautéed beef or lamb cooked with onions, tomatoes, and spices. The flavorful meat mixture is then wrapped in thin lavish bread and served with a squeeze of lemon juice.

Sac Kavurma:

⬚ Sac Kavurma is a delicious meat dish made with tender chunks of lamb or beef cooked on a hot metal plate called a "sac." The meat is seasoned with spices and often accompanied by onions, peppers, and tomatoes. The sizzling meat is served hot and is best enjoyed with freshly baked bread.

Karides Guvec:

⬚ Antalya's coastal location makes it an ideal place to indulge in seafood dishes. Karides Guvec is a delectable shrimp casserole cooked with tomatoes, peppers, onions, garlic, and a variety of herbs and spices. The dish is baked in a clay pot, allowing the flavors to meld together, resulting in a rich and aromatic seafood delight.

Manti:

- Manti is a popular Turkish dumpling dish that can be found throughout the country, including Antalya. The dumplings are small and filled with a mixture of ground meat, onions, and spices. They are typically served with a garlicky yogurt sauce and topped with melted butter and a sprinkle of sumac or chili flakes.

Etli Ekmek:

- Etli Ekmek, which translates to "meat bread," is a thin, crispy flatbread topped with a mixture of ground lamb or beef, onions, peppers, and tomatoes. It is cooked in a wood-fired oven until the meat is perfectly tender and the bread is golden and crunchy. Etli Ekmek is a popular street food dish that satisfies both meat and bread cravings.

Baklava:

- No visit to Antalya is complete without indulging in some traditional Turkish sweets. Baklava is a classic dessert made of layers of flaky filo pastry filled with a sweet mixture of nuts, usually pistachios or walnuts, and held together with sweet syrup. The combination of buttery pastry and the richness of the nut filling creates a heavenly treat.

Sütlaç:

- Sütlaç is a delightful Turkish rice pudding made with milk, sugar, rice, and a hint of vanilla. The pudding is cooked slowly until the rice becomes tender and the mixture thickens. It is then baked until the top forms a golden crust. Sütlaç is often served chilled and garnished with a sprinkle of cinnamon or crushed pistachios.

These are just a few of the many delicious dishes that Antalya has to offer. Don't hesitate to explore the local restaurants and street food stalls to discover even more culinary delights during your visit.

Traditional Restaurants and Cafes in Antalya

Antalya is home to a variety of traditional restaurants and cafes that offer a taste of authentic Turkish cuisine and a glimpse into the local culture. Here are some establishments where you can experience the traditional flavors and ambiance of Antalya:

Seraser Fine Dining Restaurant:

- Seraser is a renowned fine dining restaurant located in the heart of

Antalya's old town, Kaleici. It offers a sophisticated setting with a charming courtyard and serves traditional Turkish dishes prepared with a modern twist. The menu features a variety of meat and seafood specialties, mezze (appetizers), and delectable desserts.

Seven Mehmet Restaurant:

- Seven Mehmet is a popular traditional restaurant situated in the historic district of Kaleici. It is known for its warm and cozy atmosphere, complete with Ottoman-style décor. The restaurant specializes in classic Turkish dishes, such as lamb kebabs, stuffed vine leaves, and savory pastries. Live music performances add to the lively ambiance.

Yemenli Restaurant:

⬚ Yemenli is a family-owned restaurant located in Kaleici that has been serving traditional Turkish cuisine since 1981. The restaurant offers a wide range of mezze, kebabs, and grilled seafood. Diners can enjoy their meals in a relaxed and welcoming environment with attentive service.

Tarihi Karaf Bistro Café:

⬚ Tarihi Karaf is a charming café located in the Kaleici area. It occupies a restored historic building and offers a cozy and intimate setting. The café serves a variety of Turkish breakfast options, including freshly baked pastries, olives, cheeses, and traditional Turkish tea. It's a perfect spot to start your day with a leisurely breakfast.

Köy Sofrası Restaurant:

⊠ Köy Sofrası, meaning "village table," is a rustic restaurant situated in a picturesque village setting near Antalya. It focuses on serving traditional Turkish cuisine made with locally sourced ingredients. The menu includes hearty dishes like slow-cooked stews, grilled meats, and traditional village bread. The restaurant also offers panoramic views of the surrounding countryside.

Antalya Balık Evi:

⊠ If you're a seafood lover, Antalya Balık Evi is a must-visit restaurant. Located near the harbor, it specializes in fresh seafood dishes prepared in the traditional Turkish style. From grilled fish to seafood mezzes, you can savor the flavors of the Mediterranean while enjoying views of the sea.

Antalya Şekerleme Tatlısı:

- For those with a sweet tooth, Antalya Şekerleme Tatlısı is a delightful traditional sweets shop. It offers a wide selection of Turkish desserts, including baklava, Turkish delight, and various pastries. Treat yourself to these delectable treats accompanied by a cup of Turkish tea or coffee.

Antalya Kaleiçi Kahvesi:

- To experience the traditional Turkish coffee culture, visit Antalya Kaleiçi Kahvesi. Located in the heart of Kaleici, this café offers a cozy and authentic setting where you can enjoy a cup of rich Turkish coffee prepared in the traditional way. Pair it with a slice of Turkish delight for a true Turkish coffee experience.

These traditional restaurants and cafes in Antalya provide not only delicious meals but also a glimpse into the local culture and culinary heritage.

Whether you're seeking fine dining, cozy cafés, or rustic village-style eateries, these establishments offer a range of options to satisfy your cravings and provide a memorable dining experience.

Culinary Delights in Antalya

Antalya is a paradise for food lovers, offering a wide array of culinary delights that showcase the rich flavors and traditions of Turkish cuisine. From succulent kebabs to mouthwatering sweets, here are some culinary delights you must try during your visit to Antalya:

Adana Kebab:

- Adana Kebab is a famous Turkish kebab originating from the city of Adana. It consists of skewered and grilled minced lamb or beef, seasoned with a blend of spices, including red pepper flakes, paprika, and cumin. The kebab is traditionally served with flatbread, grilled vegetables, and a side of yogurt.

Lahmacun:

　Lahmacun, often referred to as "Turkish pizza," is a thin and crispy dough topped with a mixture of minced lamb or beef, tomatoes, onions, and a variety of herbs and spices. It is baked in a hot oven and served with fresh lemon wedges and parsley. Roll it up and enjoy the burst of flavors in every bite.

Meze:

　Meze refers to a variety of small appetizers that are served before the main course. Antalya offers a wide selection of meze options, including haydari (yogurt with herbs and garlic), acılı ezme (spicy tomato and pepper dip), patlıcan salatası (eggplant salad), and yaprak sarma (stuffed grape leaves). Enjoy the combination of flavors and textures as you sample different meze dishes.

Manti:

- Manti is a beloved Turkish dish that consists of tiny dumplings filled with a mixture of ground meat, onions, and spices. The dumplings are boiled and served with a garlicky yogurt sauce and drizzled with melted butter and a sprinkle of sumac or chili flakes. Each bite offers a burst of flavors that will leave you craving for more.

Turkish Tea and Coffee:

- Turkish tea, known as çay, is an integral part of Turkish culture. Served in small tulip-shaped glasses, it is a fragrant and refreshing drink enjoyed throughout the day. Turkish coffee, on the other hand, is strong and rich, brewed in a cezve (a small pot) and served with a side of lokum (Turkish delight). Experience the art of tea and coffee drinking in the traditional Turkish style.

Baklava:

⬜ Baklava is a famous Turkish dessert made of layers of thin and flaky filo pastry, filled with a sweet mixture of finely chopped nuts (such as pistachios or walnuts) and held together with a sweet syrup made from honey or sugar. The combination of buttery pastry, crunchy nuts, and sweet syrup creates a heavenly treat that will satisfy your sweet tooth.

Dondurma:

⬜ Dondurma, also known as Turkish ice cream, is a unique and stretchy ice cream made with milk, sugar, and salep (a type of flour derived from orchid roots). It has a distinct texture and elasticity, which makes it different from regular ice cream.

Enjoy the playful and entertaining experience of watching the dondurma vendors perform tricks with the ice cream while savoring its delicious flavors.

Pide:

⬧ Pide is a Turkish-style flatbread topped with various ingredients and baked in a hot oven. It is similar to pizza but with a distinct Turkish twist. The toppings can include cheese, ground meat, vegetables, or a combination of flavors. Pide is best enjoyed fresh out of the oven, with its crispy crust and flavorful toppings.

These culinary delights in Antalya will take you on a journey of flavors and introduce you to the rich culinary heritage of Turkey. Don't miss the opportunity to savor these delicious dishes and experience the vibrant food scene that makes Antalya a true culinary destination.

VIII. Shopping and Souvenirs

Old Bazaar (Kaleici Pazari) in Antalya

The Old Bazaar, also known as Kaleici Pazari, is a vibrant and bustling marketplace located in the heart of Antalya's historic district, Kaleici. Steeped in history and culture, this lively bazaar offers a treasure trove of goods, from traditional crafts and local products to spices, textiles, and souvenirs. Here's what you can expect when exploring the Old Bazaar:

Traditional Turkish Crafts and Souvenirs:

- The Old Bazaar is a haven for those seeking traditional Turkish crafts and souvenirs. Browse through an array of stalls and shops offering handmade ceramics, carpets, kilims, copperware, glassware, and wooden handicrafts. Take the opportunity to find unique gifts or keepsakes to remind you of your time in Antalya.

Authentic Turkish Delights and Spices:

- As you wander through the Old Bazaar, you'll encounter shops filled with colorful displays of Turkish delights, spices, and teas. Indulge your taste buds with a variety of mouthwatering Turkish sweets, such as lokum (Turkish delight), baklava, and helva. Don't forget to explore the aromatic spices, including saffron, cumin, sumac, and dried herbs, which add a touch of Turkish flavor to your culinary adventures.

Antiques and Vintage Finds:

⬚ The Old Bazaar is a paradise for antique enthusiasts and collectors. Antique shops and stalls offer a fascinating collection of vintage items, including jewelry, coins, traditional clothing, old maps, and intricate Ottoman-era artifacts. Delve into the past as you uncover hidden treasures and immerse yourself in the rich history of the region.

Handwoven Textiles and Carpets:

117

- Turkey is renowned for its handwoven textiles and carpets, and the Old Bazaar is an ideal place to admire and purchase these exquisite creations. Explore shops that showcase a range of beautiful rugs, kilims, and tapestries in various patterns and colors. Learn about the art of carpet weaving and, if desired, find the perfect piece to adorn your home.

Leather Goods:

- Antalya is known for its quality leather products, and the Old Bazaar offers a fantastic selection of leather goods. From jackets, bags, and belts to shoes and accessories, you'll find an assortment of leather items crafted with skill and care. Browse through the shops, feel the softness of the leather, and treat yourself to a stylish and enduring souvenir.

Traditional Turkish Tea Houses and Cafes:

⬚ Amidst the shopping excitement, take a break and unwind at one of the traditional Turkish tea houses or cafes scattered throughout the Old Bazaar. Enjoy a cup of Turkish tea or coffee while soaking up the vibrant atmosphere, watching the hustle and bustle of the marketplace. It's a perfect opportunity to relax, people-watch, and savor the local ambiance.

Local Cuisine and Delicacies:

⬚ The Old Bazaar is not only a shopping destination but also a culinary adventure. Explore the food stalls and small restaurants offering a variety of local delicacies. Taste traditional Turkish street food like simit (sesame-covered bread rings), gözleme (stuffed savory pancakes), and freshly squeezed fruit juices. Allow your senses to be tantalized by the aromas and flavors of Turkish cuisine.

Historical Architecture and Atmosphere:

⬚ The Old Bazaar is nestled within the winding streets and historic buildings of Kaleici, providing a charming and nostalgic atmosphere. Immerse yourself in the architectural beauty of Ottoman-era houses, mosques, and ancient city walls. As you stroll through the narrow alleys, admire the fusion of history, culture, and commerce that defines the Old Bazaar.

The Old Bazaar in Antalya's Kaleici district offers a vibrant and enchanting shopping experience. Whether you're seeking traditional crafts, unique souvenirs, or immersion into Turkish culture and cuisine, the Old Bazaar is a must-visit destination that will leave you with unforgettable memories of your time in Antalya.

Shopping Malls in Antalya

In addition to the traditional markets and bazaars, Antalya is home to several modern shopping malls that offer a diverse range of international brands, entertainment options, and dining experiences. Whether you're in search of high-end fashion, electronics, or leisure activities, here are some prominent shopping malls in Antalya:

TerraCity Shopping Mall:

 TerraCity is one of the largest and most popular shopping malls in Antalya. Located in the Lara district, it houses a wide range of international and Turkish brands, including fashion, cosmetics, electronics, and home goods. The mall features a spacious layout, indoor and outdoor areas, a food court, and a cinema complex.

MarkAntalya Shopping Mall:

⬥ Situated in the heart of Antalya, MarkAntalya Shopping Mall offers a convenient shopping experience with a diverse selection of shops. From fashion and accessories to electronics and household items, the mall caters to various shopping preferences. It also features a food court, restaurants, and a cinema for additional entertainment.

Deepo Outlet Center:

⬥ Deepo Outlet Center is a popular destination for bargain hunters and those looking for discounted branded goods. Located near Antalya Airport, it offers a wide range of international and Turkish brands at discounted prices. The mall has a village-style layout and features a variety of shops, cafes, and restaurants.

Migros 5M Shopping Mall:

- Migros 5M is a large shopping mall situated on the outskirts of Antalya. It is part of the Migros retail chain and offers a comprehensive shopping experience. The mall includes a hypermarket, fashion stores, electronics shops, and a food court. It also features a children's play area and entertainment facilities.

ÖzdilekPark Shopping Mall:

- ÖzdilekPark Shopping Mall is located in the Konyaalti district of Antalya and offers a mix of international and Turkish brands. The mall features a spacious interior, a variety of shops, a food court, and entertainment options. It is a popular destination for both locals and tourists.

Mall of Antalya:

⧄ Mall of Antalya is a modern and stylish shopping mall located in the Muratpaşa district. It houses a wide range of national and international brands, including fashion, electronics, and home decor. The mall features a contemporary design, spacious walkways, a food court, and a multiplex cinema.

Agora Shopping Center:

⧄ Agora Shopping Center is a smaller-scale mall situated in the Konyaalti district of Antalya. It offers a selection of shops, including fashion, accessories, and household goods. The mall also features a supermarket, restaurants, and cafes, providing convenience for shoppers.

S'hemall Shopping Mall:

⧄ S'hemall is a shopping mall located in the Muratpaşa district of Antalya. It offers a range of shops, including fashion, electronics, and home furnishings. The mall provides a modern and comfortable environment for shopping, dining, and entertainment.

These shopping malls in Antalya provide a contemporary and convenient shopping experience, with a variety of international and Turkish brands to choose from. Whether you're in search of fashion, or electronics, or simply want to explore the vibrant atmosphere of a modern mall, Antalya's shopping malls have something for everyone.

Local Handicrafts and Artisanal Products in Antalya

Antalya is known for its rich cultural heritage, and a visit to the city provides an opportunity to explore and appreciate the local handicrafts and artisanal products created by skilled artisans. From traditional crafts to unique souvenirs, here are some local handicrafts and artisanal products you can discover in Antalya:

Traditional Carpets and Kilims:

- Antalya is renowned for its exquisite handwoven carpets and kilims. These intricate textiles are created using traditional techniques passed down through generations. Visit carpet shops and workshops to witness the craftsmanship firsthand and find unique rugs and kilims that showcase traditional designs and vibrant colors.

Ceramics and Pottery:

- Antalya's pottery and ceramics reflect the region's artistic heritage. Skilled artisans create beautiful pieces, such as decorative plates, vases, bowls, and tiles, using traditional methods. Look for workshops or studios where you can observe the pottery-making process and purchase one-of-a-kind ceramic pieces as souvenirs or for home decoration.

Turkish Mosaic Lamps:

◻ Turkish mosaic lamps are iconic and eye-catching pieces of art. These colorful lamps are made by hand, with intricate patterns of colored glass pieces meticulously assembled to create stunning lighting fixtures. Explore shops and stalls specializing in mosaic lamps to find a unique piece that adds a touch of Turkish ambiance to your home.

Leather Goods:

◻ Antalya is known for its high-quality leather products. Skilled artisans craft a wide range of leather goods, including jackets, bags, wallets, belts, and shoes. The leather is carefully worked and finished to create durable and stylish products. Look for shops or boutiques that offer authentic leather goods and select a piece that suits your style.

Traditional Jewelry:

 Traditional Turkish jewelry is renowned for its intricate designs and fine craftsmanship. Explore jewelry stores and boutiques to find a variety of pieces, including intricately detailed silver necklaces, bracelets, rings, and earrings adorned with gemstones or traditional motifs. Each piece tells a story and serves as a beautiful memento of your time in Antalya.

Glassware:

 Antalya boasts a tradition of glassmaking, producing unique and colorful glassware. Look for hand-blown glass products, such as decorative bowls, vases, and ornaments, that showcase the artistry and craftsmanship of local glass artists. These vibrant pieces can serve as beautiful decorations or thoughtful gifts.

Traditional Turkish Textiles:

◻ Traditional Turkish textiles, such as handwoven towels, scarves, and shawls, are highly sought after for their quality and intricate designs. Explore shops and stalls to find a wide range of textiles made from natural fibers like cotton and silk. These textiles can be used as functional items or displayed as decorative elements in your home.

Olive Oil and Local Food Products:

◻ Antalya is known for its high-quality olive oil production. Look for shops that offer locally produced olive oil, as well as other food products like spices, jams, and dried fruits. These items not only make for delicious culinary souvenirs but also provide a taste of the region's flavors and culinary traditions.

When exploring the local handicrafts and artisanal products in Antalya, take the time to engage with the artisans and learn about the techniques and stories behind their creations. By supporting these skilled craftsmen and women, you contribute to the preservation of traditional crafts and take home unique pieces that embody the spirit of Antalya's cultural heritage.

IX. Nightlife and Entertainment

Bars and Clubs in Antalya

Antalya offers a vibrant nightlife scene with a variety of bars and clubs catering to different tastes and preferences. Whether you're seeking a relaxing evening at a cozy bar or a night of dancing and entertainment at a lively club, here are some popular options in Antalya:

Kaleici Bars:

- The historic district of Kaleici is known for its charming bars and pubs. Wander through the narrow streets and discover cozy establishments offering a laid-back atmosphere. Enjoy a cocktail or a local Turkish beer while taking in the ambiance of this picturesque neighborhood.

Marina Bars:

  ▢ Antalya Marina is a hub for nightlife with a selection of bars offering scenic views of the harbor and the Mediterranean Sea. Whether you prefer a trendy rooftop bar or a waterfront lounge, you'll find a variety of options to enjoy a drink and socialize in this lively area.

Live Music Venues:

  ▢ Antalya boasts several live music venues where you can enjoy performances by local bands and musicians. From jazz and blues to rock and traditional Turkish music, these venues offer an opportunity to immerse yourself in the local music scene while enjoying a drink or two.

Beach Clubs:

  ▢ Antalya's stunning coastline is dotted with beach clubs that offer a unique nightlife experience. These clubs provide a combination of sun, sand, music, and entertainment. Lounge on comfortable beach beds during the day and transition into a vibrant party atmosphere as the sun sets.

Nightclubs:

⬚ Antalya is home to a variety of nightclubs that cater to different music genres and styles. From electronic dance music to Turkish pop, you'll find clubs with energetic atmospheres and talented DJs. Dance the night away and enjoy the energetic vibes of these nightlife hotspots.

Open-Air Bars:

⬚ Take advantage of Antalya's warm climate and enjoy open-air bars that offer refreshing cocktails and a relaxed atmosphere. These bars often have outdoor seating areas with comfortable lounges or rooftop terraces, providing a perfect setting to unwind and socialize.

Karaoke Bars:

 ⊠ If you're in the mood for some interactive entertainment, Antalya has karaoke bars where you can showcase your singing skills or enjoy the performances of others. Sing your favorite tunes and join in the fun at these lively venues.

Irish Pubs and Sports Bars:

 ⊠ For those looking for a taste of home or a place to watch live sports events, Antalya has Irish pubs and sports bars that offer a cozy and familiar atmosphere. Enjoy a pint of beer, catch a game, and socialize with fellow travelers or locals in these welcoming establishments.

It's important to note that the nightlife scene in Antalya may vary depending on the season and current regulations. It's always a good idea to check the opening hours and any specific requirements before visiting bars and clubs. Enjoy the diverse nightlife offerings in Antalya, but remember to drink responsibly and respect local customs and regulations.

Live Music Venues in Antalya

Antalya offers a vibrant live music scene with venues that showcase talented local musicians and bands. Whether you're a fan of jazz, rock, traditional Turkish music, or international sounds, here are some popular live music venues in Antalya:

The Corners Jazz Club:

- The Corners Jazz Club, located in the heart of Antalya, is a popular destination for jazz enthusiasts. This cozy and intimate venue hosts live jazz performances by local and international artists. Sit back, relax, and immerse yourself in the smooth sounds of jazz in a stylish and inviting atmosphere.

Route Antalya:

 Route Antalya is a music and performance venue that showcases a variety of genres, including rock, pop, indie, and alternative music. With its state-of-the-art sound system and dynamic atmosphere, Route Antalya attracts both local and touring bands. Experience live music performances and discover new talent in this energetic setting.

Antalya Arena Amphitheatre:

 The Antalya Arena Amphitheatre is a unique outdoor venue that hosts concerts and live performances during the summer months. With its stunning acoustics and historical ambiance, this ancient amphitheater provides an unforgettable setting for live music events featuring a diverse range of genres and artists.

Piano Bar at Titanic Deluxe Golf Belek:

 The Piano Bar at Titanic Deluxe Golf Belek offers a sophisticated and elegant setting for live music performances. Enjoy the soothing melodies of live piano music while sipping on your favorite drink. The bar features a relaxed atmosphere, making it an ideal spot to unwind and enjoy a night of musical entertainment.

The Doors Pub:

 The Doors Pub is a popular live music venue in Antalya known for its energetic atmosphere and diverse music lineup. From rock and blues to reggae and pop, this venue hosts local bands and musicians who deliver high-energy performances. Dance the night away or simply enjoy the lively ambiance of The Doors Pub.

Sahne Park Antalya:

- Sahne Park Antalya is an open-air venue located in the heart of Antalya that hosts live music events and concerts. With its spacious outdoor area and stage, Sahne Park attracts both local and international artists. From pop and rock to traditional Turkish music, this venue offers a diverse range of musical performances.

Captain's Place Pub:

- Captain's Place Pub is a lively and popular establishment that features live music performances by local musicians. Located in the Kaleici district, this pub offers a cozy atmosphere where you can enjoy a drink, socialize, and listen to a variety of genres, including rock, pop, and blues.

Moonlight Park & Beach Club:

⊠ Moonlight Park & Beach Club is a multi-purpose entertainment venue that hosts live music events and concerts during the summer season. Located on Konyaalti Beach, this beach club offers a scenic setting with a stage that overlooks the sea. Enjoy live performances by local and international artists while enjoying the beachside atmosphere.

These live music venues in Antalya provide a platform for talented musicians and offer music enthusiasts a chance to experience the vibrant local music scene. Check the schedules and upcoming events to plan your visit and enjoy the diverse range of musical genres and performances in Antalya.

Cultural Performances in Antalya

Antalya is a city rich in cultural heritage, and experiencing traditional performances is a fantastic way to immerse yourself in the local culture. From traditional Turkish dances to music and theatrical productions, here are some cultural performances you can enjoy in Antalya:

Whirling Dervishes:

- The Whirling Dervishes performance is a mesmerizing display of Sufi spiritual tradition. The dancers, dressed in flowing white robes, engage in a meditative spinning dance called "Sema." This captivating performance combines music, poetry, and whirling movements that symbolize the spiritual journey of attaining unity with the divine.

Turkish Folk Dance Shows:

⬚ Turkish folk dance shows showcase the vibrant and diverse regional dances of Turkey. Performers adorned in colorful costumes bring to life traditional dances from different regions, such as the energetic Zeybek dances from Western Anatolia or the lively Horon dances from the Black Sea region. Experience the rhythmic movements and lively music that depict the cultural heritage of Turkey.

Live Turkish Music Performances:

⬚ Enjoy live performances of traditional Turkish music that showcase various musical instruments and genres. From the haunting melodies of the ney (reed flute) to the enchanting sounds of the oud (lute) and kanun (zither), immerse yourself in the rich musical traditions of Turkey. Live music performances often feature talented musicians who captivate audiences with their skill and passion.

Antalya State Symphony Orchestra:

 The Antalya State Symphony Orchestra is a renowned musical ensemble that offers classical music performances throughout the year. Experience the power and beauty of symphonic compositions and enjoy captivating concerts that feature both local and international musicians.

Aspendos Opera and Ballet Festival:

 The Aspendos Opera and Ballet Festival is an annual cultural event held in the ancient Aspendos Theater near Antalya. This prestigious festival showcases opera and ballet performances by national and international artists. The spectacular setting of the well-preserved ancient theater adds a unique ambiance to the performances.

Antalya Culture and Arts Festival:

◻ The Antalya Culture and Arts Festival is a multi-disciplinary festival that celebrates various art forms, including music, dance, theater, and visual arts. Held in different venues throughout the city, the festival features performances by local and international artists, providing a vibrant showcase of cultural diversity.

Antalya State Theater:

◻ The Antalya State Theater presents a range of theatrical productions, including dramas, comedies, and musicals. Enjoy performances by talented actors who bring captivating stories to life on stage. The theater showcases both traditional Turkish plays and international productions.

Mevlana Cultural Center:

◻ The Mevlana Cultural Center in Antalya hosts a variety of cultural events, including music concerts, dance performances, and theater productions. This cultural hub promotes artistic expression and offers a platform for local and international artists to showcase their talent.

These cultural performances in Antalya provide an opportunity to appreciate the rich traditions, music, and performing arts of Turkey. Check the schedules and venues to plan your attendance and witness the captivating performances that celebrate the cultural heritage of Antalya.

Cultural Performances in Antalya

Antalya is a city that celebrates its rich cultural heritage through a variety of captivating performances. From traditional dances to music and theatrical productions, here are some cultural performances you can experience in Antalya:

Traditional Turkish Dance:

- Traditional Turkish dance performances showcase the vibrant and diverse dance styles of Turkey. From the energetic and rhythmic movements of the folk dances to the elegant and precise steps of the Ottoman court dances, these performances bring to life the cultural traditions and stories of the region.

Mevlevi Sema Ceremony:

- The Mevlevi Sema ceremony, also known as the Whirling Dervishes, is a deeply spiritual and mesmerizing performance. The dancers, dressed in white robes, perform a ritualistic spinning dance as a form of worship and meditation. It is a unique opportunity to witness this ancient Sufi practice and experience the spiritual atmosphere it creates.

Live Turkish Music:

- Enjoy live performances of traditional Turkish music that showcase a range of instruments, including the oud (lute), ney (reed flute), and kanun (zither). Experience the melodic tunes and captivating rhythms that reflect the rich musical heritage of Turkey. Whether it's classical Turkish music or contemporary interpretations, these performances provide an immersive musical experience.

Antalya State Symphony Orchestra:

- The Antalya State Symphony Orchestra is a renowned ensemble that presents classical music performances throughout the year. Experience the grandeur and emotion of symphonies, concertos, and other orchestral works performed by talented musicians. The orchestra's performances provide a memorable experience for lovers of classical music.

Antalya Culture and Arts Festival:

▯ The Antalya Culture and Arts Festival is a yearly event that celebrates various art forms, including music, dance, theater, and visual arts. The festival brings together local and international artists who showcase their talent through performances and exhibitions. It's an excellent opportunity to immerse yourself in the cultural scene of Antalya.

Antalya State Theater:

▯ The Antalya State Theater presents a range of theatrical productions, including classic and contemporary plays, musicals, and experimental works. Enjoy the art of storytelling and witness the creative interpretations of talented actors and directors. The theater offers a diverse program that caters to different theatrical tastes.

Aspendos Opera and Ballet Festival:

🔲 The Aspendos Opera and Ballet Festival is a prestigious event held annually in the ancient Aspendos Theater near Antalya. It features breathtaking opera and ballet performances by national and international artists. The combination of world-class performances and the historic setting of the theater creates a magical experience.

Local Folk Performances:

🔲 Explore local cultural centers and venues that host folk performances representing the diverse regions of Turkey. These performances showcase traditional costumes, music, and dances specific to different parts of the country. It's an opportunity to witness the richness and diversity of Turkish folk culture.

Immerse yourself in the cultural performances of Antalya and witness the beauty, grace, and passion that these artistic expressions convey. Check the schedules and venues to plan your attendance and enjoy the captivating cultural performances that make Antalya a vibrant cultural destination.

X. Practical Information and Tips

Local Customs and Etiquette in Antalya

When visiting Antalya, it's important to be aware of and respectful of the local customs and etiquette. Here are some tips to help you navigate the cultural norms and ensure a positive and enjoyable experience:

Greetings and Politeness:

- When meeting locals, it is customary to greet them with a handshake and a warm smile. Use "Merhaba" (hello) or "Selam" (hi) when addressing people. It is polite to address older individuals with a title such as "Bey" (Mr.) or "Hanim" (Mrs./Ms.) followed by their last name.

Dress Code:

- Antalya is a popular tourist destination, and while it is generally more relaxed in terms of dress code, it is advisable to dress modestly, especially when visiting religious sites and in more conservative areas. Cover your shoulders and avoid wearing revealing clothing in such contexts.

Religious Etiquette:

▯ Antalya has a diverse religious landscape, and it's important to respect religious sites and customs. When entering mosques, remove your shoes and dress modestly. Women may be required to cover their heads with a scarf. Avoid loud conversations or disruptive behavior in religious spaces.

Hospitality and Politeness:

▯ Turkish people are known for their hospitality and friendliness. Accepting an invitation to someone's home is considered an honor, and it's polite to bring a small gift such as chocolates or flowers. When visiting someone's home, remove your shoes at the entrance unless otherwise indicated.

Dining Etiquette:

▯ When dining with locals, it is customary to wait for the host or elder to start eating before you begin. It's polite to taste a bit of everything on your plate and avoid leaving food uneaten. If offered tea or coffee, it's customary to accept the gesture and engage in conversation while enjoying your drink.

Public Displays of Affection:

⬚ Public displays of affection, such as kissing or hugging, are generally more reserved in Turkey compared to some other cultures. It's advisable to show restraint and be mindful of local norms when it comes to physical affection in public.

Tipping:

⬚ Tipping is a common practice in Antalya. In restaurants, it's customary to leave a tip of around 10% of the total bill, although some establishments may include a service charge. Tipping is also expected for other services, such as taxi rides and hotel staff assistance.

Cultural Sensitivity:

☒ Antalya is a multicultural city with visitors from around the world. It's important to be sensitive to different cultural backgrounds and avoid making assumptions or engaging in stereotypes. Embrace diversity and be open to learning about different perspectives.

Language:

☒ While many people in Antalya speak English, it's appreciated when visitors make an effort to learn a few basic Turkish phrases. Simple greetings and expressions of gratitude in Turkish can go a long way in showing respect for the local language and culture.

Bargaining:

☒ Bargaining is a common practice in markets and bazaars in Antalya.

However, it's important to do so respectfully and with a friendly attitude. Engage in light-hearted negotiations, but also be mindful of the value and quality of the item you are bargaining for.

By being aware of and respecting the local customs and etiquette, you will create positive interactions and forge meaningful connections with the people of Antalya. Embrace the cultural differences and enjoy your time in this beautiful city while fostering mutual understanding and respect.

Health and Safety in Antalya

Antalya is generally a safe destination for travelers, but it's always important to prioritize your health and safety during your visit. Here are some tips to help ensure a safe and enjoyable stay in Antalya:

Travel Insurance:

☒ Before your trip to Antalya, it's advisable to have travel insurance that covers medical expenses, trip cancellations, and lost or stolen belongings. Familiarize yourself with the coverage details and keep a copy of your insurance information readily available.

Vaccinations and Medical Precautions:

☒ Check with your healthcare provider or travel clinic well in advance to determine if any vaccinations or preventive medications are recommended for your visit to Antalya. Make sure your routine vaccinations are up to date, including measles, mumps, rubella, diphtheria, pertussis, tetanus, and influenza.

Safe Drinking Water:

⊠ It is recommended to drink bottled water or use filtered water for drinking and brushing your teeth. Avoid consuming tap water, including ice cubes, from unknown or unreliable sources to prevent water-borne illnesses.

Sun Protection:

⊠ Antalya has a Mediterranean climate with hot summers. Protect yourself from the sun by wearing sunscreen with a high SPF, a hat, sunglasses, and lightweight, breathable clothing. Seek shade during the peak hours of intense sunlight, usually between 10 a.m. and 4 p.m.

Personal Safety:

⊠ As with any destination, it's important to take basic precautions to ensure personal safety. Be aware of your surroundings, especially in crowded places or tourist areas. Keep an eye on your belongings and use a secure bag or money belt to prevent theft. Avoid displaying excessive amounts of cash or valuable items in public.

Local Laws and Customs:

- ▢ Familiarize yourself with the local laws and customs of Antalya to ensure you respect and comply with them. Pay attention to any specific regulations regarding dress codes, photography restrictions, and behavior in religious or cultural sites.

Transportation Safety:

- ▢ When using public transportation or taxis, choose reputable providers and be cautious of potential scams. Follow traffic rules if renting a vehicle, and consider using authorized transportation services for airport transfers or day trips.

Emergency Contacts:

◻ Keep a list of important emergency contacts, including local authorities, your embassy or consulate, and your travel insurance provider. It's also a good idea to have a copy of your passport and other important documents stored in a secure location.

COVID-19 Precautions:

◻ Stay informed about the latest COVID-19 guidelines and restrictions in Antalya. Follow recommended safety measures, such as wearing masks in public spaces, practicing social distancing, and regularly sanitizing your hands. Stay updated on travel advisories and requirements before and during your trip.

Remember that these guidelines are general recommendations, and it's always advisable to stay informed about the specific health and safety conditions in Antalya during your visit. Stay vigilant, trust your instincts, and enjoy your time exploring the beauty and culture of Antalya while prioritizing your well-being.

Useful Phrases

Here are some useful phrases in Turkish that can come in handy during your visit to Antalya:

Greetings:

- Hello: Merhaba
- Good morning: Günaydın
- Good evening: İyi akşamlar
- Goodbye: Hoşça kal

Polite Expressions:

- Please: Lütfen
- Thank you: Teşekkür ederim
- You're welcome: Rica ederim

- Excuse me: Affedersiniz
- I'm sorry: Özür dilerim

Basic Conversations:

- Yes: Evet
- No: Hayır
- How are you?: Nasılsınız?
- I'm fine, thank you: İyiyim, teşekkür ederim
- What is your name?: Adınız ne?
- My name is [your name]: Benim adım [your name]

Directions and Transportation:

- Where is...?: ...nerede?
- Can you help me?: Bana yardım edebilir misiniz?
- How much does it cost?: Ne kadar?
- I want to go to...: ...game istiyorum
- Is it far?: Uzak mı?

Ordering Food and Drinks:

- I would like...: ...istiyorum
- Menu: Menü
- Water: Su

- Coffee: Kahve
- Bill, please: Hesap, lütfen

Emergency Situations:

- Help!: Yardım edin!
- I need a doctor: Bir doktora ihtiyacım var
- Where is the nearest hospital?: En yakın hastane nerede?
- Call the police: Polisi arayın

Shopping:

- How much is it?: Ne kadar?
- Can I try it on?: Deneyebilir minim?
- Do you have this in a different color/size?: Bunun farklı bir range/been var mı?
- I would like to buy this: Bununla almak istiyorum

Remember that attempting to speak a few basic phrases in the local language can go a long way in showing respect and building connections with the locals. Don't hesitate to ask for help or clarification if needed, as many people in Antalya are friendly and willing to assist you.

Recommended Travel Resources

When planning your trip to Antalya, here are some recommended travel resources that can provide useful information and assistance:

Official Tourism Websites:

- Visit Antalya (www.visitantalya.com): The official tourism website for Antalya provides comprehensive information about attractions, accommodations, events, and transportation options in the city.
- Ministry of Culture and Tourism of the Republic of Turkey

(www.kultur.gov.tr): The official website of the Ministry of Culture and Tourism offers valuable information about travel destinations, cultural heritage, and tourism policies in Turkey.

Travel Guides:

- Lonely Planet Turkey: A well-known travel guidebook that provides detailed information on attractions, accommodations, transportation, and practical tips for travelers visiting Turkey, including Antalya.

- Rick Steves' Istanbul: Rick Steves' guidebook focuses on Istanbul, but it also covers other popular destinations in Turkey, including Antalya, providing insightful travel advice and recommendations.

Online Travel Forums and Communities:

- TripAdvisor (www.tripadvisor.com): An online platform where you can read reviews, get recommendations, and ask questions in the Antalya travel forum to get insights from fellow travelers and local experts.

⊠ Lonely Planet's Thorn Tree Forum (www.lonelyplanet.com/thorntree): An online forum where you can interact with other travelers, ask questions, and share experiences about traveling to Antalya and other destinations in Turkey.

Local Transportation Information:

⊠ Antalya Metropolitan Municipality (www.antalya.bel.tr): The official website of the Antalya Metropolitan Municipality provides information about public transportation services, including bus routes, schedules, and fares within the city.

⊠ Antalya Airport (www.antalya-airport.aero): The official website of Antalya Airport offers flight information, airport facilities, transportation options to and from the airport, and other useful details for air travelers.

Travel Apps:

    ▪ Google Maps: A reliable navigation app that can help you find your way around Antalya, locate attractions, restaurants, and hotels, and provide real-time transportation information.

    ▪ XE Currency: A currency converter app that allows you to quickly convert currencies and stay updated with the latest exchange rates.

These resources can assist you in planning your trip, finding reliable information, and staying informed about important details during your visit to Antalya.

Printed in Great Britain
by Amazon

27211681R00096